P9-EDY-861

STEPHEN CURRY
BASKETBALL'S MVP

Therese M. Shea

Enslow Publishing
101 W. 23rd Street
Suite 240
New York, NY 10011
w.com

Words to Know

average A number that is figured out by adding a set of figures together and dividing the sum by the number of figures.

draft The process of selecting new players to enter a sports league.

hustle To play a sport with great effort.

injury A wound.

malaria A sometimes deadly disease spread by mosquitoes.

physical Involving a lot of bodily contact.

point guard In basketball, the guard who is responsible for directing a team's play when they possess the ball.

tournament A sports event made up of a series of games or rounds.

unanimous In complete agreement.

varsity The main team that represents a school.

CONTENTS

Words to Know......................2

Chapter 1 Born Athlete...................... 5

Chapter 2 The College Game.............. 8

Chapter 3 A Warrior........................... 12

Chapter 4 True MVP.......................... 16

Timeline 22

Learn More 23

Index.................................. 24

BORN ATHLETE

Stephen (STEF-in) Curry may be the best shooter in NBA history. Without a doubt, he is an NBA champion, an MVP, and a player who has just begun to play at the top of his game.

Stephen was born March 14, 1988, in Akron, Ohio. His real name is Wardell Stephen Curry II, though he goes by Stephen or Steph. His father is Dell Curry, who was an NBA player himself. His mother, Sonya, was a star volleyball player at Virginia Tech, where Dell also attended. Sports were always

FUN FACT

Stephen wears the number 30 on his jersey in honor of his father, who wore the number 30 when he played for the Charlotte Hornets.

Stephen's father, Dell, played in the NBA from 1986 to 2002. In a 1992 photo, a young Stephen sits on his father's lap.

an important part of Stephen's life.

The Currys lived mostly in Charlotte, North Carolina, after Dell signed with the Charlotte Hornets. Stephen played basketball in the family's backyard with his younger brother, Seth, as kids. They learned much by watching their father play, but they also learned the importance of working hard from their mother.

Stephen's mother started an elementary school, which he attended.

VARSITY PLAYER

Stephen later enrolled at Charlotte Christian

Stephen Says:

"We'd play for hours and hours, oftentimes well into the night with the use of a bright stage light shining on the court, until our mom would yell out the window for us to come."

High School, where his talent on the court began to shine—but not at first. As a freshman, he was too short and hadn't yet proved his skill. When he was finally called up to **varsity** during a state **tournament**, he wowed the coach with a three-pointer and earned a spot on the team. He worked hard to keep his spot with early morning workouts and by studying opponents. Said his coach, "Every year he brought something new to his game. And that was truly just a function of him working."

During Stephen's time at Charlotte Christian, the team went to the state tournament three times. He graduated as the school's all-time leading scorer and a two-time All-State honoree.

Stephen's brother, Seth, became an NBA player, too. Their sister, Sydel, is a star volleyball player.

CHAPTER 2
THE COLLEGE GAME

Stephen hoped to play for Virginia Tech, where his father and mother attended. However, the coaches did not think there was a spot for Stephen on their team. Other schools believed Stephen was too short, though he had grown to be 6 feet (1.8 meters) tall!

FUN FACT
If Stephen didn't play basketball, he would probably be playing golf. Not only does he love the game, he's good at it, too! He played with President Obama in 2015.

Coach Bob McKillop of Davidson College in North Carolina, knew there was something special about Stephen. Besides being a point scorer, McKillop saw a player who could be tough and physical. He also recognized Stephen's focus and willingness to hustle. Davidson was a small school, but the team played

Bob McKillop said he could tell that Stephen wanted to do more than score points. He wanted to master every part of the game.

Stephen Says:

"It was . . . a dream realized to be sitting in the green room with my family hearing my name called as the seventh overall pick of the NBA Draft."

against many respected teams. Stephen agreed to attend and play for Davidson.

SCORING AS A WILDCAT

Stephen's effect on the Davidson Wildcats was immediate. He was named Southern Conference Freshman of the Year. His sophomore year brought him national attention when he led Davidson to the regional finals of the NCAA tournament—the Elite Eight. Davidson nearly upset Kansas, the team that went on to become the champions.

In his junior year, Stephen perfected his point guard skills. He averaged 28.6 points per game, totaling 974 points, the most of any Division I player. Stephen decided to enter the 2009 NBA Draft. He was chosen in the first round by the Golden State Warriors.

By the time he made the pros, Stephen had grown to be 6 foot 3 (1.9 m)!

CHAPTER 3
A WARRIOR

Stephen was a standout his first pro year, averaging 17.5 points, 5.9 assists, and 1.9 steals. He was second place for NBA Rookie of the Year. He was also named to the men's national team, helping the United States win gold at the 2010 FIBA World Championships.

FUN FACT

In the 2012 season, Stephen scored an average of more than 22 points per game. He holds the single-season record for the most three-pointers made in an NBA season.

Highlights of the 2010–2011 NBA season include owning the best free-throw percentage in the league and winning the All-Star Weekend Skills Challenge and the NBA Sportsmanship Award.

Unfortunately, **injuries** took Stephen out of much of the 2011–2012 season. Some were unsure if the Warriors should re-sign him. The team took a chance, and Stephen made them glad they did.

ALL-STAR PLAYER

In the 2012–2013 season, Stephen achieved some personal bests. He sunk 272

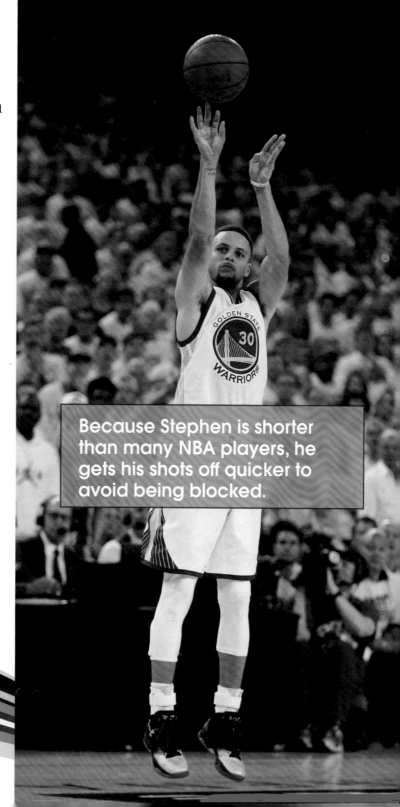

Because Stephen is shorter than many NBA players, he gets his shots off quicker to avoid being blocked.

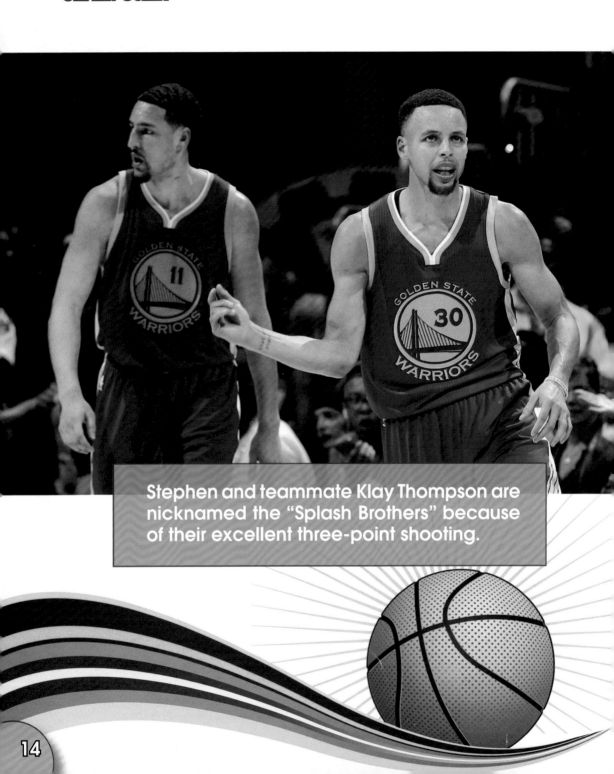

Stephen and teammate Klay Thompson are nicknamed the "Splash Brothers" because of their excellent three-point shooting.

three-pointers, the most in the NBA. The Warriors made it to the play-offs but lost in the second round.

In 2013–2014, Stephen broke the Warriors' record for most career three-pointers and also topped the league with 261. He was also selected as an All-Star for the first time. Golden State again made the play-offs but lost in the first round.

Stephen Says:

"Make it work no matter what you have to work with—that's something that stuck with me very early on as a point guard. Adjust. Get creative. Try a different angle, a different lane, a different move, or a different shot—just make it work."

CHAPTER 4
TRUE MVP

The 2014–2015 season was amazing for both the Golden State Warriors and their point guard. Stephen smashed his own record for regular-season three-pointers with 286. He averaged 23.8 points per game and led the NBA in steals with 163.

This performance earned Stephen the NBA Most Valuable Player (MVP) Award. It also meant a trip to the play-offs, where the Warriors met the Cleveland Cavaliers in the finals. The Warriors won the championship for the first time in forty years.

In 2015–2016, Stephen Curry again led the league in three-point shots, with an incredible 402. He was named MVP once again, the first player to win by unanimous vote. The Golden State Warriors set a record as well. They won more regular-season games than any NBA team

Stephen Says:

"I love that basketball gives me the opportunities to do good things for people."

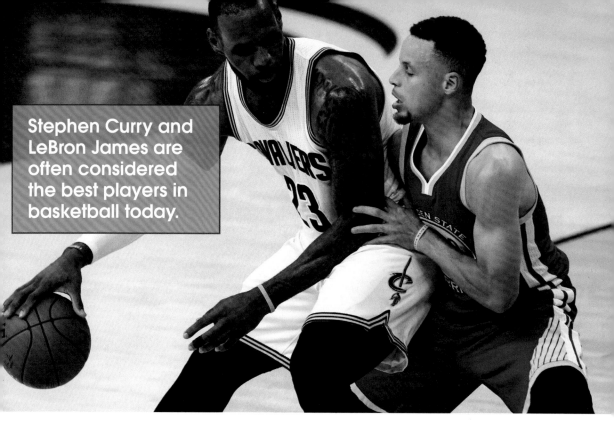

Stephen Curry and LeBron James are often considered the best players in basketball today.

ever, with 73 wins and only 9 losses. The Warriors and the Cavaliers again met in the NBA finals, but only one could be named champion. LeBron James went on to lead the Cleveland Cavaliers in victory against Stephen Curry and the Golden State Warriors.

Stephen was invited to play at the 2016 Olympic Games in Rio de Janeiro, Brazil. However, he decided to take the off-season to rest so he would be in the best shape possible for the next season.

FUN FACT

Riley Curry is a young media darling. She often appears with her father at the post-game press conferences. She is also often featured on her mother's Instagram account.

A FAMILY MAN

Stephen is known to always be willing to pose for a photo or sign an autograph. He credits his family with keeping him down to earth. He married Ayesha Alexander in 2011, and they have two daughters, Riley and Ryan.

Stephen and his family give back to their community. The Stephen Curry Foundation raises money for schools

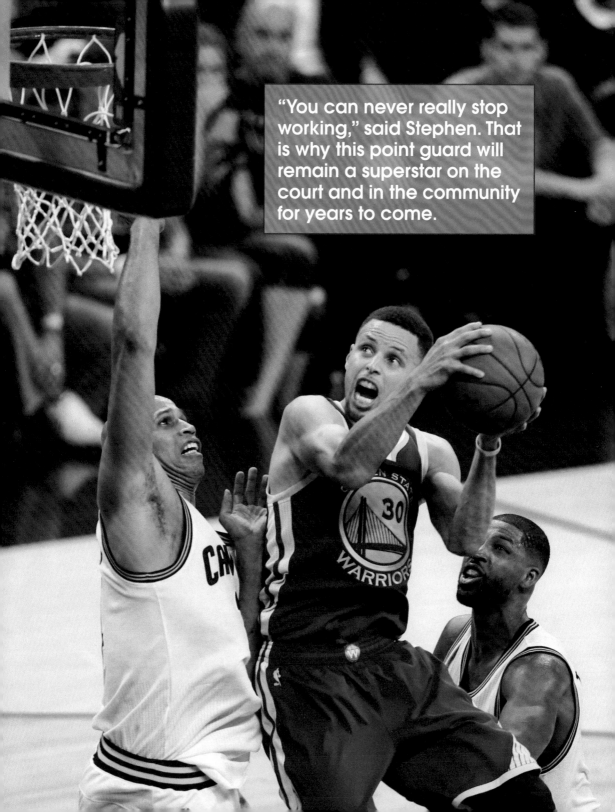

"You can never really stop working," said Stephen. That is why this point guard will remain a superstar on the court and in the community for years to come.

The Curry family is very close. Dell (*behind Stephen*), comes to many of his son's games with Stephen's wife Ayesha (*right*), and their two daughters Riley (*held by Stephen*) and Ryan.

in need. Stephen also works with the Nothing But Nets charity, which donates mosquito nets to battle malaria in Africa. He donates three nets for every three-pointer he sinks. That is quite a large number for the three-point champion!

It is certain that Stephen Curry's career has only just begun. His strengths as a team leader, a player, and a family man will surely make him an invaluable player for many years to come.

TIMELINE

1988 Wardell Stephen Curry II is born March 14 in Akron, Ohio.

2006 Stephen begins attending Davidson College.

2008 Davidson goes to the Elite Eight in the NCAA tournament.

2009 Stephen is chosen as the seventh pick in the NBA Draft by the Golden State Warriors.

2010 Stephen wins a gold medal with the US National Team at the FIBA World Championships.

2011 Stephen marries Ayesha Alexander.

2013 Stephen tops the league in three-pointers.

2015 Stephen is named NBA MVP. The Warriors win the NBA Championship.

2016 Stephen again wins the MVP Award but the Warriors lose to the Cavaliers in the NBA finals.

LEARN MORE

Books

Fishman, Jon M. *Stephen Curry*. Minneapolis, MN: Lerner Publications, 2016.

Schuh, Mari. *Stephen Curry*. North Mankato, MN: Capstone Press, 2016.

Wilner, Barry. *The Best NBA Shooters of All Time*. Minneapolis, MN: Abdo Publishing, 2015.

Websites

Basketball Reference
basketball-reference.com/players/c/curryst01.html
All of Stephen Curry's stats can be found here.

Biography.com
www.biography.com/people/stephen-curry
Read a short biography of the NBA superstar.

Stephen Curry
stephencurry30.com
Check out Stephen's official website.

INDEX

C

Charlotte Christian High School, 6–7
Cleveland Cavaliers, 16–17
Curry, Ayesha Alexander, 18
Curry, Dell, 5, 6, 8
Curry, Riley and Ryan, 18
Curry, Seth, 6
Curry, Sonya, 5, 6, 8

D

Davidson College, 8–10

G

Golden State Warriors, 10, 12–15, 16–17

J

James, LeBron, 17

M

McKillop, Bob, 8
MVP Award, 5, 16

N

NBA Draft, 10

O

Nothing But Nets, 21

Olympics, 18

S

Stephen Curry Foundation, 18–21

T

three-pointers, 7, 15, 16, 21

V

Virginia Tech, 5, 8

Published in 2017 by Enslow Publishing, LLC.
101 W. 23rd Street, Suite 240, New York, NY 10011

Library of Congress Cataloging-in-Publication Data
Names: Shea, Therese, author.
Title: Stephen Curry : basketball's MVP / Therese M. Shea.
Description: New York : Enslow Publishing, 2017. | Series: Junior Biographies | Includes bibliographical references and index.
Identifiers: LCCN 2016020790| ISBN 9780766081758 (Library Bound) | ISBN 9780766081734 (Paperback) | ISBN 9780766081741 (6-pack)
Subjects: LCSH: Curry, Stephen, 1988—Juvenile literature. | Basketball players—United States—Biography—Juvenile literature.
Classification: LCC GV884.C88 S47 2017 | DDC 796.323092 [B] — dc23
LC record available at https://lccn.loc.gov/2016020790

Printed in China

To Our Readers: We have done our best to make sure all websites in this book were active and appropriate when we went to press. However, the author and the publisher have no control over and assume no liability for the material available on those websites or on any websites they may link to. Any comments or suggestions can be sent by e-mail to customerservice@enslow.com.

Photo Credits: Cover, p. 1 John W. McDonough/Sports Illustrated/Getty Images; pp. 4, 7, 13, 19, 20 Ezra Shaw/Getty Images; p. 6 © (1992) NBA Entertainment, Photo by Andrew D. Bernstein/NBAE/Getty Images; p. 9 Raleigh News & Observer/Tribune News Service/Getty Images; p. 11 Jim McIsaac/Getty Images; p. 14 Kevin C. Cox/Getty Images; p. 17 Jason Miller/Getty Images; back cover, pp. 2, 3, 22, 23, 24 (curves graphic) Alena Kazlouskaya/Shutterstock.com; interior pages (basketball graphic) pop jop/DigitalVision Vectors/Getty Images.